Looking at Norse Myths and Legends

The Giant King

Rosalind Kerven

BRITISH MUSEUM PRESS

Rosalind Kerven is a trained anthropologist who now works as a full-time writer and reviewer of children's books. She has published numerous volumes of myths, legends and folk-tales, including *Looking at Celtic Myths and Legends: Enchanted Kingdoms* (British Museum Press, 1997)

Published by British Museum Press
A division of The British Museum Company
46 Bloomsbury Street, London WC1B 3QQ

A catalogue record for this book is available from the British Library

ISBN 0 7141 2112 6

Designed by Carla Turchini
Printed in Hong Kong

Front cover: Head of a warrior, carved from antler, found at Sigtuna, Sweden.

Contents

About these stories 5

Names and places 7

A Journey To Giant Land 8

Don't Play With Giants! 32

Further reading 46

Sources of the pictures 47

ASGARD

YGGDRASILL

BIFROST BRIDGE

UTGARD

JOTUNHEIM

MIDGARD
(Middle Earth)

JORMUNGAND

NIFLHEL

About these stories

These stories come from the Viking Age, which started about 1,200 years ago (in the eighth century AD) and lasted for 300 years. They were told by the Norse people of Denmark, Norway and Sweden. These people were great adventurers and explorers. Many of them went to live in Britain, Ireland and other parts of Europe, as well as Iceland and Greenland, taking their stories with them.

The Norse myths were part of the old religion followed by these people before they became Christians. Unfortunately, we know very little about how this religion was practised. However, we can tell from the stories that they believed in many different gods and goddesses. Some of them seem to have helped and protected their followers, but others were always rather dangerous. The most important and mysterious god was Odin, the 'All-Father', while the most popular was Thor, the thunder god. Loki, the trickster god, was probably the strangest, and certainly the most mischievous.

The gods and goddesses lived in a world called Asgard. When they wanted to visit the world of people, they walked down a flaming rainbow bridge called Bifrost to Midgard (Middle Earth). This was surrounded by a vast ocean, and beyond the sea lay the land of giants, Jotunheim. Far below Middle Earth was Niflhel, the world of the dead. These three worlds were connected by a gigantic ash-tree called Yggdrasill.

In many ways the Norse gods and goddesses were like human beings, but they were much more colourful and extreme, and they had various magical powers. There were also giants, dwarves, trolls and elves. Stories such as the ones in this book tell how such beings often mixed their adventures and conflicts into the lives of ordinary people – often with very surprising results!

Names and places

Asgard	The home of the gods
Bifrost bridge	The rainbow bridge linking Asgard and Middle Earth
Honir	A god who helped create human beings
Jormungand	The World Snake, who lay coiled around Middle Earth
Jotunheim	The Land of the Giants
Loki	The trickster god
Midgard or Middle Earth	The home of human beings
Mjollnir	Thor's great hammer
Niflhel	The underworld, land of the dead
Odin	The 'All-Father', wisest and most mysterious of the gods
Skrymir	The king of the giants
Thialfi and Roskva	Two children, brother and sister
Thor	The mighty thunder god
Utgard	The fortress of the giant king
Yggdrasill	The great ash tree linking all the worlds

A Journey To

Unexpected Visitors

There were once two children who lived in Middle Earth: Roskva was the girl and her brother was called Thialfi. Their home was a poor farm in a wild and lonely place.

One night they were startled to hear the noise of wheels and hooves stopping outside their hut and then men's voices, calling loudly.

'Go and see who it is,' said their mother.

Giant Land

They opened the door. Outside stood a chariot, pulled by two big billy-goats – and sitting inside it were two extraordinary men.

One of these men was really big and strong, with thick muscles rippling in his hairy arms. His russet-red beard was thick and bristly. The gloves on his huge hands were made of solid iron. His belt sizzled and sparkled and he carried a heavy hammer carved with strange runes and patterns.

The other man was lean and small, finely dressed and handsome. He was beardless, with smooth skin like a woman or a snake. His dark, penetrating eyes danced here and there; his mouth was alive with smiles.

Roskva and Thialfi stood there, staring. The lean man winked at them.

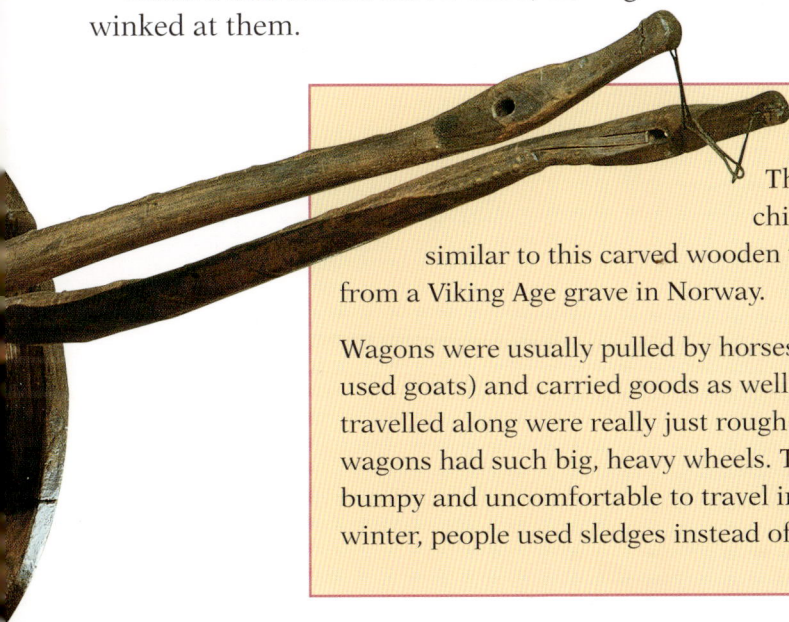

The chariot in which Thor and Loki arrived at the children's farm may be similar to this carved wooden wagon, which was dug up from a Viking Age grave in Norway.

Wagons were usually pulled by horses or oxen (although Thor used goats) and carried goods as well as people. The roads they travelled along were really just rough tracks, which is why the wagons had such big, heavy wheels. They must have been very bumpy and uncomfortable to travel in. During the snows of winter, people used sledges instead of wagons.

'Who are you?' whispered Roskva, shrinking away.

At once, the big man burst out laughing. His laugh was so loud that the children jumped and their parents came out, running.

'What?' he boomed, 'don't tell me you really don't know us!' He nudged his companion and roared with laughter again. 'Me, I'm Thor – the Thunderer they call me. This lizard-like creature is my side-kick, Loki. We're on our travels, you see. This is a bleak, unfriendly place you live in! Yours is the first house we've come to for miles. You can see it's getting dark. We want you to give us a warm bed for the night.'

The children's mother swallowed her nervousness. 'You'd better come in, my lords,' she said. 'You're welcome – very welcome. Only as you can see, we're rather poor and we haven't got much to offer you. There's nothing for supper tonight except for a small pot of thin soup.'

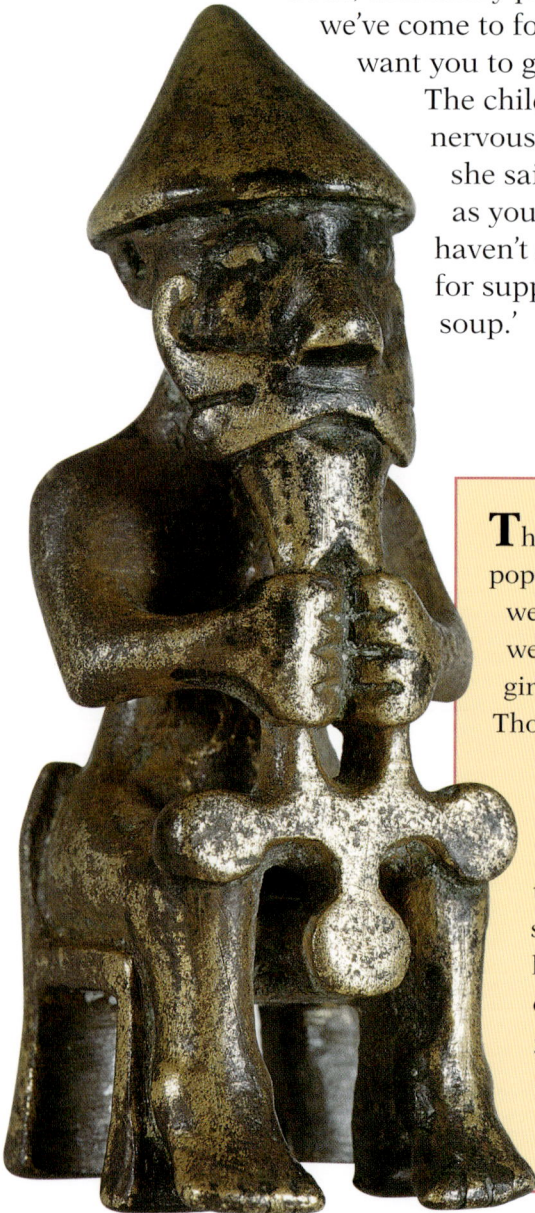

Thor, the god of thunder, was the most popular of all the Norse gods. Many people were named after him. Typical boys' names were Thord, Thorgeir and Thorkel, while girls might be called Thorgerd, Thorhalla or Thorkatla. Even today, we remember Thor's name in the word 'Thursday'.

The stories tell us that Thor had an enormous palace with 540 rooms, and that he loved eating and drinking. He was strong and brave and always stuck up for his friends; but he could be very fierce and dangerous to his enemies, especially the giants. He is shown here holding his great hammer. You can see another picture of Thor's hammer on page 18.

The two gods followed her into the little turf house: the children and the farmer came in behind. It was a squash with them all in there and rather stuffy, but the fire glowed nice and cosy and warm.

Loki pulled off his boots and stretched himself out on the floor beside the flames with a sigh of contentment. He said in a reedy voice:

'Why don't you do your meat-trick for them, Thor?'

Thor cleared his throat. 'Ah, good idea,' he said. 'You, boy,' (this was to Thialfi) 'pop outside and unhitch my two goats, will you? Then bring them in here to me.'

Thialfi brought in the goats. Then Thor took his knife, cut the animals' throats, skinned them, sliced them into hunks of meat, and threw them into the farm-woman's cooking pot.

'We'll eat them tonight,' he said, 'then tomorrow I'll bring them back to life. It won't do them any harm.' He beamed round at them kindly. 'Enjoy it! Eat as much as you want. But *make sure you don't break any of the bones.* Just throw them onto the goatskins over there when you've finished with them, and leave them to me.'

The meat was soon cooked. Fresh goat meat from the gods' pastures: it was the most delicious meal any of them had ever eaten!

The farm-woman, her husband and Roskva all took great care to put the bones to one side, as Thor had told them to.

But Loki fixed Thialfi with his dark, shifty eye and grinned.

The boy caught Loki's thought. He turned his back on the others and secretly took out his knife. He sliced open a big thigh-bone and sucked out the rich, juicy marrow. Then, without a word, he threw the broken bone onto the pile.

Night came and everyone slept. Then it was morning. The two gods made themselves ready to be on their way.

Thor took his hammer. He held it out over the dead goat-skin and bones, whispering magic words. At once, the two goats both became whole and alive again! But now one of them was lame.

Loki pointed his finger at Thialfi. 'The boy did it,' he said. 'He disobeyed you, Thor, and broke a bone. I saw him! Punish him!'

When archaeologists examined the face carved on this stone, they noticed that there were lines carved across its closed mouth. Because of this, they guessed that the face is probably Loki. He was punished in one story by having his lips sewn together.

Loki was the strangest and most dangerous of all the gods, half-good and half-evil. He was attractive, clever and charming – but he was also very devious and loved playing cruel tricks on people. It was always safest not to trust Loki, for he took great delight in getting people into terrible trouble – even his friends.

Thor looked at the goat, and glowered at Thialfi. His face darkened and he roared: 'You'll have to pay me compensation for this!'

'But my lord,' cried the boy's mother, trembling, 'we've got nothing to pay you with! You've seen how poor we are. I know our son's been a bad boy, terribly bad, but ...'

Meanwhile Loki was wheedling at Thor, whispering in his ear. 'Why don't you take *him*? Make them pay you with the boy himself!'

At once Thor's roar changed into laughter. 'Ho, that's a good one! Yes, lady, I'll take your son for compensation – and his pretty little sister too, for good measure. We'll swap them for the goats and chariot. Good thinking, Loki. They can be our slaves, and help us out on the journey.'

'But ... but where are you going?' asked the woman.

Loki gave her a dazzling smile. 'To Utgard,' he said, 'in the Land of the Giants!'

Noises in the Forest

So Roskva and Thialfi travelled with the gods, walking on and on until they reached a stony beach that ran down to the sea. There they found a boat, and climbed into it.

Thor rowed the boat strongly across the grey water. When they landed on the other side, they were in Jotunheim, the Land of the Giants.

At first sight, this land did not look much different from Middle Earth. However, there was an icy chill in the air, and the distant mountains were wrapped in white, drifting mist.

'Come on,' cried Thor, 'let's go and find some giants! I want to show them once and for all, that the gods are much better than they are. If it comes to it, I'm all ready for a fight!' And swinging his hammer cheerfully around his head, he led the way up from the shore.

Soon they found themselves in the middle of a vast forest. The trees were very fat and tall and covered in wispy fronds of moss and lichen like dwarf-beards. There seemed to be no end to them in any direction.

Deeper and deeper into the forest the travellers went, always following Thor. At last the sun turned orange and sank behind the dark trees: night fell.

'Look!' cried Thialfi, 'there's a house!'

Sure enough, through the trees, they saw a building – but it was a very odd one. The entrance into it was as tall and wide as the house itself, and there was no door to pull shut across it. It was built of a very peculiar material: not wood, not stone, not turf ... instead, the walls, the roof and even the floor were all made of something soft and leathery. Inside there was just one huge, empty room, with a very high ceiling. A narrow tunnel led off to one side, but when they explored it, it went nowhere.

Still, they had to find somewhere to sleep, and this was better than nothing. So they all went in, and began to make themselves comfortable. First, at Thor's command, Thialfi laid out some bear-fur sleeping rugs. Then Roskva passed around some of the food left over from their goat-meat feast. There was more than enough for all of them. When they had all eaten as much as they could, they lay down and went to sleep.

Everything was fine for a while. But in the middle of the night they were all woken suddenly by a dreadful, bone-chilling noise. *Rrr..ch...chwaa...arr...rrrr!!* It sounded like the battle-cry of a giant pig with indigestion. And at the very same moment the ground beneath them began to shudder and judder and buckle and toss.

'Help!' screamed Loki, jumping up and grabbing Roskva and Thialfi as if he expected them to protect him. 'Earthquakes! Enemies! Avalanches! Save us, Thor!'

Thor was on his feet at once, brandishing his hammer. 'Don't worry, don't panic,' he boomed. Instantly, both the noises and the shuddering stopped.

They all held their breath. Everything was quiet and still. Then suddenly again:

Rrr..ch...chwaa...arr...rrrr!!

Shudder, judder, shake!

'Quick,' said Thor, 'all of you – get into that tunnel. You'll be safe in there from whatever it is. I'll stand on guard at the entrance with my hammer for the rest of the night. Don't worry: not even the fiercest monster can get past my thunderbolts.'

So the others crept away into the dark, narrow tunnel that led to nowhere. Loki went in first, lurking in the shadows at the far end where it was safest. Then came Roskva and Thialfi. At the entrance, Thor stood firmly on guard.

All night long there were many more noises, many more shudderings on and off and on. But at last morning came, and it grew light.

Off went Thor, stamping his way outside to find out what was happening. Loki and the children followed him. They hadn't gone very far when they saw a huge giant!

The giant was as tall, thick and gnarled as an old oak tree.

Myths tell how the giants were the first living creatures. Later on the gods arrived, and forced the giants to go and live in the bleak, stormy lands of ice and snow. The rough giants never forgave the gods for this, and were always plotting to get their revenge.

Hardly any Viking Age pictures of giants still exist today. Perhaps this rather ugly silver mask was meant to show a giant's face. It was found in a Viking grave in Sweden, and is quite small. It may have been worn as a pendant on a necklace.

He lay stretched out on the ground, fast asleep, snoring.
    'Rrrr...ch..chwa...arr..rrr!' went his snores; and the whole forest shook.

So that was what they had heard with such fear and trembling, all last night!

'Stand back,' commanded Thor. 'I'll soon deal with this monster.'

He raised his hammer, all ready to strike a mighty blow – but before he could do so, the giant suddenly sat up, rubbing his eyes.

'Well, well, well, if it isn't old Thor!' he exclaimed, holding out his enormous hand in a very friendly way. 'I heard you were coming, you old Thunderer. Pleased to meet you!'

Slowly, suspiciously, Thor put down his hammer. 'And who are you?' he asked gruffly.

'Skrymir's my name,' said the giant, peering at the other three with interest. 'By the way, have any of you seen my glove? I lost it somewhere round here last night ... Ah, but look, there it is!'

He pointed straight towards the strange house they had just left. They all turned to stare at it. Sure enough, they could see now that it really was a huge glove – a glove big enough to fit Giant Skrymir's hand. (The dark tunnel where they had hidden was actually the hole for his thumb.)

Loki narrowed his eyes and sucked in his lips. 'That was a neat trick, Skrymir,' he said.

'It takes one trickster to admire an even better one,' laughed Skrymir. 'But listen, my friends, you've seen nothing yet! Where is it you're going?'

'To the fortress of Utgard,' said Thor.

'Oh-hoh, Utgard is it?' said Skrymir. 'Then I'll come with you some of the way.' He grinned down at them. 'It seems to me that little ant-sized creatures like you need a bit of help and protection when you travel through Giant-Land. Come on, let me carry that heavy pack of food for you. I'll lead the way.'

And before they could stop him, he had picked up their pack and was striding off into the trees.

Strong Thongs

Skrymir took such long, fast strides that Thor, Loki and Roskva were soon left far behind. Only Thialfi managed to keep up, for the boy was a really fast runner. Every so often he went racing ahead to see where Skrymir had got to, and then back to the others to show them the way.

'I'm glad I brought him,' said Thor to Loki. 'His speed might prove very handy while we're here.' But Loki was more interested in thinking about his stomach. 'Run and tell Giant Skrymir we're all starving,' he said to Thialfi. 'Tell him to stop and open the pack for our picnic.'

Thialfi ran ahead with this message. When he heard it, the giant grunted, sat down and tossed the pack onto the ground.

'Tell Thor to open it himself,' he said. 'It's nothing to do with me.'

Then he lay back and fell into another deep, snoring sleep.

The other three caught them up, and Thialfi told them what Skrymir had said. Thor grabbed the pack and, with his strong, hairy fingers, began to untie the thongs that were holding it tightly shut.

'Hurry up,' said Loki, watching impatiently. His stomach was rumbling.

Thor began to growl. Then he cursed. Then he began to shout with rage.

'The filthy worm! He's put some kind of magic on these thongs! They're impossible to open!'

'You can't let him get away with this,' hissed Loki.

'No, I can't and I won't!' cried Thor. He turned round and glared at the sleeping giant. Then he raised his hammer and straight away brought it down phutt! onto Skrymir's head.

The children jumped back and clutched each other. Loki grinned. Thor stood breathing heavily, stroking his hammer and waiting.

'HO!' All of a sudden, Skrymir sat up. 'Phew,' he said. 'I was having such a lovely dream – and then something disturbed me. It must have been a leaf fluttering down. I only felt a sort of tickle.' He smiled at them. 'Enjoying your picnic?' Then he went straight back to sleep.

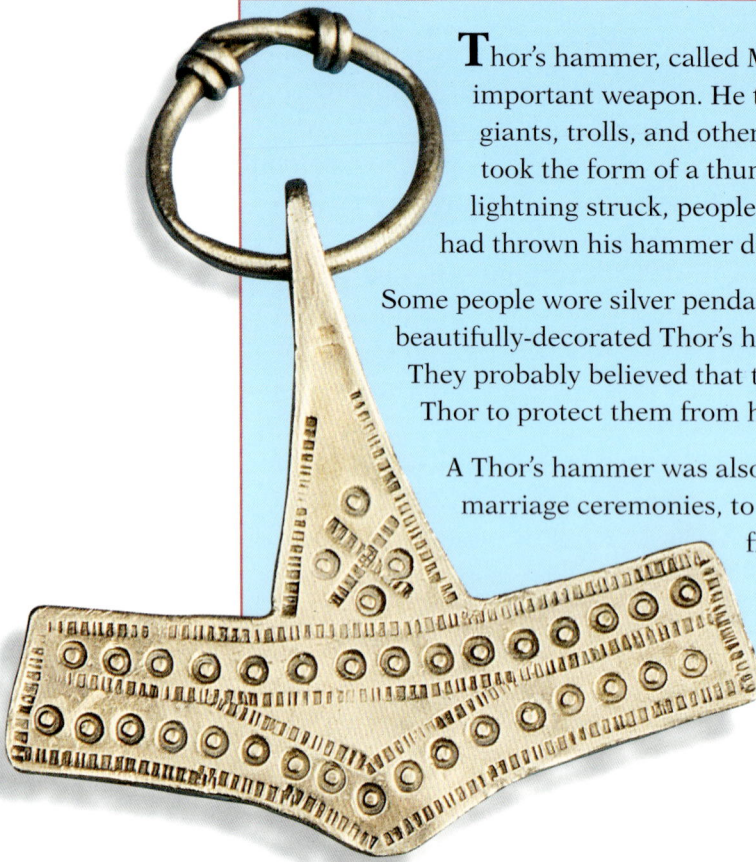

Thor's hammer, called Mjollnir, was his most important weapon. He threw it or used it to hit giants, trolls, and other enemies. Sometimes it took the form of a thunderbolt. When lightning struck, people used to say that Thor had thrown his hammer down to earth.

Some people wore silver pendants shaped into beautifully-decorated Thor's hammers, like this one. They probably believed that this would encourage Thor to protect them from harm.

A Thor's hammer was also used in Viking Age marriage ceremonies, to keep evil powers away from the newly-weds, and bring them lots of children.

Thor's face was nearly as red as his beard. 'All of you,' he cried, 'help me!'

He began to tug at the thongs again. Loki tried to bite through them. Roskva scratched at them with her sharp finger-nails. Thialfi tried to cut them with his knife.

'It's no good,' said Thor at last. 'Ordinary strength is useless against giant magic. I'll just have to use my hammer on the villain until I can make him see sense.'

He stepped back and gave the giant another great whack on the head with his hammer.

'AH!' Skrymir woke up again. 'What a nuisance: now an acorn seems to have fallen on me. That's the trouble, sleeping out here in the open. Hmmm ... Hey, you lot, isn't it time for your beddy-byes?'

Before they could answer, he lay back, closed his eyes and began to snore again.

'There's nothing for it,' whined Loki. 'We'll just have to go to bed hungry.' He curled up on the ground like an animal and went straight to sleep.

Thor shook his head gloomily. 'He's right, you know,' he told the children. 'Let's all try to sleep now. I'll have another bash at Skrymir in the morning.'

So they all lay down and dozed on the hard ground. As dawn began to break, Roskva and Thialfi woke up and saw Thor standing over the giant, taking aim with his hammer for the third time.

Crash! The hammer came down with a really hard blow, and sank deep into Skrymir's head.

'Dear me! Whatever was that?' Skrymir sat bolt upright and blinked around at them, rubbing his head. 'Ach, now a nasty lump of bird-muck seems to have fallen on me. I don't think I'll be camping outside again, after all this disturbance.' He yawned. 'But what about you four? Did you all enjoy your picnic last night? Did you sleep well?'

They were all dumbstruck, even Thor and Loki.

'Not very talkative this morning, are you?' said Skrymir, getting up and stretching. 'Never mind, I was about to say goodbye to you, anyway. I have to take a different path from here. But if you lot are really determined to go as far as Utgard, you'll have to keep on along the same way we were going. Mind you, if you decided to turn back and go home before you run into any more trouble, I wouldn't call you cowards.'

'What do you mean, sir?' whispered Roskva.

'Well,' said Skrymir, 'I can see you're all sneaking looks at me, and thinking I'm a pretty tough nut, eh? But as I warned you yesterday, you haven't seen anything yet! Once you get to Utgard, you'll meet giants who'll make me seem like a dainty little water-sprite! Listen, Thor, let me give you some advice: save your hammer from any more failures, and lead your tiny friends home to safety while you still can.'

'Never!' cried Thor. 'No-one sends Thor the Thunderer back from his chosen path! Everyone knows the gods are mightier than the giants! I'm on my way to Utgard to make my mark there, and I'm not going back until I've done it!'

Skrymir shrugged. 'Please yourself, thunder-god,' he said. And then he vanished.

The Giant King's Castle

Thor and Loki, Roskva and Thialfi walked on, trying to forget how hungry they were. As the sun rose high in the sky, the forest thinned out and they found themselves standing outside a massive fortress. Its walls were so high that the tops were lost in the clouds.

The gates were made of iron bars, each one as thick as a man's leg. There was no key to open them, and no guard to let the travellers in.

'Stand back!' cried Thor, and he smashed his hammer hard against the bars. But it did not even make a tiny dent, the iron was so tough. Next, Thor put the bulging muscles of his shoulder to the gates and tried to force them apart; but he could not budge them at all.

Loki pushed Thor aside. 'Watch,' he said.

He stood sideways and held his breath. It seemed that he was withdrawing right into himself, the way a slug can. Soon, he had shrunk enough to slip through a gap between the bars. 'Follow me,' he hissed at the others.

It was easy enough for Roskva and Thialfi – the children were already very small and thin. But mighty Thor had a really hard time of it. However much he tried to twist and draw himself in, his big, muscley body kept getting stuck. By the time Loki had dragged him right through, he was scraped and bruised all over.

But no matter, they were inside the stronghold of Utgard now, and the door into the main feasting hall stood wide open. They smoothed down their clothes, and went in.

By the bright light of hundreds of lamps, they saw a magnificent party. All down both sides of the hall, giants and giantesses were lounging around on thickly-cushioned benches, stuffing themselves with food and wine. The tables were all piled high with food. There were whole sheep's heads, roast swans with the feathers still on, bowls brim-full with cream and ruby-red berry soup, juicy joints of venison, enormous silver salmon, and many other delicious treats.

Thialfi and Roskva, Loki and Thor all felt their mouths water. But no-one offered them even a single taste.

They walked on, down the hall. Even mighty Thor looked smaller than a dwarf, compared to all those giants. Soon they came to the high-seat at the far end. In it sat the Giant King of Utgard.

'Greetings!' cried Thor in his most thunderous voice.

The Giant King peered round and then down at them, as if they were irritating insects that he could hardly see. He rubbed the end of his nose and curled up his lips; but he didn't answer.

'Hey!' boomed Thor, 'Where are your manners, Giant King? Why don't you answer me? Perhaps you don't realise who I am? Well, let me tell you. I am Thor. I am one of the greatest gods in all of Asgard!'

At these words, the Giant King's mouth twitched; and then he burst out laughing. He went on laughing until tears ran down his cheeks. He laughed so much that, although he was trying to speak, he couldn't. After a long time, he calmed down enough to splutter:

'You? But you're a mangy little maggot-sized weakling! AH-ha-ha-haa! ... I've heard all these stories, you know, about how Thor is supposed to be this amazing, big, strong god, a person to reckon with ... ha-ha-haa! ... and then you suddenly appear in front of me, claiming to be him – but looking more like a soft-skinned, half developed baby!'

Loki scowled and spat on the ground.

The Giant King ignored him. 'Anyway,' he went on, 'who said you could come sneaking into Utgard like this? We don't keep open house here, you know. Only real heroes are allowed to feast at my tables. If you don't want me to kick you out again, you'll have to prove yourselves as champions. All of you!' His eye fell on Roskva, and lingered there for a moment. 'Except the little lady, of course. She's pretty enough to please anyone. Come, sit by my foot, tiny girl-child, and watch the fun with me.'

Reluctantly, Roskva went forward and sat down on the floor next to the Giant King's boot – which was taller than her head.

'So,' said the Giant King, 'which of you fellows will offer to go first?'

Thor was still beside himself with indignation, so Loki slapped a brotherly hand on his back and stepped forward himself.

'I will.'

'You?' said the Giant King, eyeing Loki's neat, lithe form with derision. 'You don't look up to much. What can you do?'

'Eat,' said Loki, grinning and rubbing his stomach. 'I can eat more and faster than anyone.'

'Well, you look as if you could do with feeding up,' sneered the Giant King. 'For a bit of entertainment, let's try you.'

He clapped his hands for his slaves. Quickly, they came and set up a table and two stools in front of the high-seat. They gestured to Loki, who sat down at one end. To the other end came a giant whose stomach was already so fat that it wobbled and rolled every time he moved.

In front of each contestant, the slaves placed a wooden plate as big as a chariot-wheel. Each plate was piled high with all kinds of roast meat.

'Begin!' commanded the Giant King. Loki and the fat giant both began to eat.

At banquets like the Giant King's, people served food in wooden bowls and dishes, and poured drink into tankards or drinking horns. This bowl (or scoop) has a carved animal head on the handle. People ate with spoons, knives and fingers (no forks!).

The food was cooked in iron or soapstone pots, hanging over the fire on iron chains. Meat could be roasted on a spit, or cooked slowly on a hot stone. Bread was baked over hot ashes on flat iron pans.

Norse farms provided plenty of food: meat, milk, butter, soft cheese, eggs and cereals. People also ate wild nuts and berries, fish, whalemeat, wild birds and their eggs, and hunted wild boar, deer and bear for meat.

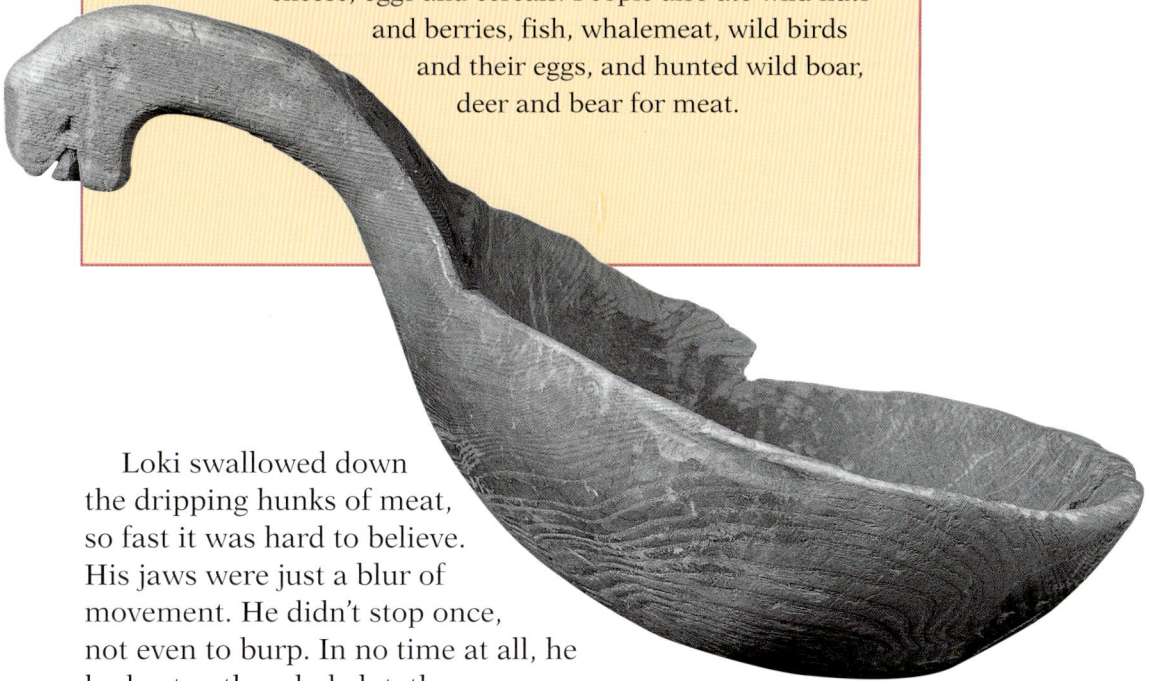

Loki swallowed down the dripping hunks of meat, so fast it was hard to believe. His jaws were just a blur of movement. He didn't stop once, not even to burp. In no time at all, he had eaten the whole lot: there was nothing left on his vast plate except for bones. He looked up in triumph.

'You've failed, Loki!' cried the Giant King. 'I knew you wouldn't stand a chance. Look at your opponent.'

Everyone turned to the other end of the table. The King was right. Not only had the fat giant eaten all his meat just as fast as Loki, but he had also gobbled down all the bones – and even the plate too!

'The giants have won the first competition,' said the King. 'Who's next?'

Loki pointed to Thialfi.

'Hmm,' said the Giant King, 'you're just an ordinary Middle Earth boy, aren't you? Still, I dare say you can't be any more pathetic than the gods. What do you want to try?'

Thialfi held his head high. 'I'll try a race,' he said. 'I can run as fast as the wind.'

'Oh,' said the Giant King, 'can you now? Well, so can one of my own lads. Hugi!' he called, snapping his fingers; and at once a young giant came up and bowed.

'You'd better do this outside,' said the Giant King. They all followed him out to a stretch of smooth, short grass behind the hall.

'Now then: ready, steady – go!'

Thialfi and Hugi raced. Thialfi ran faster than any ordinary boy had ever done before. It was as if he had turned into a hurricane: one moment he was just setting off, and the next he was already at the finishing post.

But when he looked up, he just couldn't believe it: Hugi was already there ahead of him!

'The giants have won again,' said the King. 'And now, Thor – it's your turn.'

Thor's Defeat

'What can you do?' asked the Giant King, as they went back inside.

Thor chuckled. 'Me? Oh, I'm a great drinker,' he said. 'There's no-one in all the world who's better at getting beer into his belly than I am!'

'We'll see about that,' said the Giant King. He snapped his fingers again and at once his slaves brought in a drinking-horn. This horn was so long that its end was lost in the shadows. It was filled right up to the top with frothy brown ale.

'Mmm,' said Thor, smacking his lips, this looks good.'

'I hope you can do it justice,' said the Giant King. 'There's one or two giants who can get the whole lot down in a single swig you know; not that I'd expect you to manage that, Thor – your throat's far too tiny. Two swigs wouldn't be bad. But the absolute maximum I can allow you is three swigs: if you can't empty it by then, you'll have to hang your head in shame.'

'Oh, there's no danger of that,' said Thor. He seized hold of the horn, threw back his head, and began to drink:

'Glug-ug-ug-ug-ug ....'

At last he had to stop and draw a breath. He held the horn away – and stared at it in dismay.

The Giant King coughed. 'It's still almost full.'

Thor threw him a stormy look, then drank some more, long and deep. He drew another breath. Still, the beer seemed hardly to have gone down at all.

'Last go,' remarked the Giant King.

'Glug-ug-ug-ug-ug ....'

Thor was forced to stop for breath for the third and last time. When he examined the drinking horn, he nearly exploded with rage. It was *still* almost full!

Drinking horns were made from the horns of cattle. The rim was often decorated with metal ornaments. Once it was full, the curved horn could not be put down without spilling, so it was customary to drink up all the beer, fruit-wine or mead it contained in one go. The old Norse Sagas (stories) often mention parties at which many men got drunk!

This ox-horn from Norway was probably used for drinking. It is carved with letters from the runic alphabet (you can see some more runes on pages 40-41).

'Failed,' announced the Giant King.

Thor was sweating and baring his teeth. 'This is a dirty trick!' he bellowed. 'You must have cheated me! I've never been beaten at drinking before!'

'Try him on something else,' pleaded Loki.

The Giant King looked as if he were really enjoying himself now.

'All right,' he said, 'why not? How about giving those famous muscles of yours a simple test, eh? Let's see if you can lift up my cat.'

'Your cat?' said Thor. 'By thunder, even little Roskva here could lift up a cat.'

'Not mine, she couldn't,' said the Giant King. 'Even we giants have a problem with her. Here, puss!'

A huge grey cat came slinking out, miaowing, and sat down in front of Thor.

Thor bent down and tried to lift her. He couldn't – the cat was heavier than rock. He stood up, flexed his muscles, and tried again. He *still* couldn't do it – the cat seemed glued to the floor. He grunted and groaned and roared and heaved. All the while, the cat watched him calmly from her deep, sea-green eyes.

But at last ... Thor did it! – well, just a little bit. He managed to pull one single paw, very slightly, from the ground.

The Giant King raised his eyebrows. 'Well,' he said, 'I suppose you think that's a splendid achievement, eh? I suppose you want to have a go at testing your legendary strength on something else, do you?'

Thor glowered at him darkly.

'Very well,' said the Giant King, 'how about a spot of wrestling? You can test yourself against my dear old nanny!'

At these words, a giantess, leaning heavily on a walking-stick, got up and hobbled towards the high-seat. She was very, very old. Her face was a mass of wrinkles, her back was bent, her shoulders hunched, her limbs all twisted with arthritis. She smiled, showing a black, toothless mouth.

Thor said, 'I'm sorry, I can't attack a lady. Especially not one as world-wise and ancient as you.'

'Try me,' retorted the old woman, throwing her stick to one side and holding up her fists. 'Go on, go on, don't be afraid! I'll soon tell you to stop if you're hurting.'

Thor looked doubtful. Nevertheless, he stepped forward and took a grip on the old woman; and she took a grip on him. He soon discovered that despite being all wrinkled and worn out, she was still about seven times stronger than him.

They staggered around together, huffing and puffing, straining, pushing and gasping. Then, at last, the frail old giantess pushed mighty Thor on one knee, right down to the ground, so that he had to beg for mercy.

At this, all the watching giants let out a loud cheer.

'Enough!' cried the Giant King. 'This has been a wonderful show. I've really enjoyed watching you do so badly – especially you, Thor!'

'But ...!' boomed Thor, clutching his hammer.

'You deserve a reward for making us all laugh so much,' the Giant King went on. 'Take a seat at any table you fancy, all four of you, and eat as much as you wish. Then have a good night's sleep. Tomorrow, we'll all have a talk together ...' (he winked down at Roskva) '... and I might even tell you a secret.'

The Giant King's Secrets

In the morning, the Giant King said, 'I'll show you the quickest way back through the forest. Come with me.'

Thor, Loki, Roskva and Thialfi followed him out of Utgard Castle, through the iron gates (which stood wide open now) and along a path through the trees. It was a much straighter way than they had come by, and soon they stood once more near the grey sea that separated Jotunheim from Middle Earth. They found their little boat still bobbing gently on the waves.

'My friends,' said the Giant King, 'before we say goodbye, I've got a confession to make. Listen: *I am not always what I seem to be.* And your adventures in the Land of Giants were even stranger than you think.'

'I'm not at all surprised,' Thor said grimly. 'I guessed all along that you were cheating us. Tell us everything, King – and make sure you tell the truth.'

The Giant King turned to Loki. 'Here's the first thing to tell you,' he said. 'This trickster and I share many of the same bad habits – and almost the same name. I am known in these parts as Utgard-Loki; and like you, I can be sly and clever and cunning.'

'Sly?' said Loki, preening himself. 'You might be – but I've done nothing to trick you.'

'No,' said the Giant King, 'and that's just as well for you, because my magic is always much stronger than anything the gods can manage. Let's go back over your adventures, shall we? Do you remember old Giant Skrymir, the one you met in the forest when you arrived? Remember how he thought Thor's hammer blows were just gentle tickles, when you couldn't undo your picnic? Well, he was really me in disguise!'

'So what?' asked Loki coolly.

'So keep listening. When you arrived at my palace, you were really hungry, weren't you, absolutely starving? – but you still couldn't eat as much as the giant I set against you. I'll tell you why not. He was Fire – wild Fire himself! Everyone knows that Fire always eats up absolutely everything, dead or alive, that stands in its path!'

Loki narrowed his eyes at the Giant King, and they were dark with hatred, yet aglow with a grudging admiration.

Thialfi said, 'Please your majesty, that young giant you set me to race against – who was he, really?'

'Oh, him,' said the Giant King. 'He was Thought. You went very fast my lad, very fast indeed – but everyone knows that Thought can fly faster than anything!'

'Well, well, well,' said Thor. 'So who did you put against me, you old villain?'

The Giant King stroked his beard and looked down at Thor.

'You impressed me, Thunderer,' he said. 'Right from the start, when you slammed your hammer into my head, you impressed me so much, I got quite worried.' He pointed up towards some nearby hills. 'You see those little valleys up there? They were made by your hammer blows when you thought you were hitting me. Not bad, eh? Then, when you came up to Utgard and had a go with that drinking horn, I was truly amazed that you actually managed to make some of the liquid in it completely disappear.'

'What are you talking about?' grunted Thor.

'You must have noticed that the end of the horn couldn't be seen,' said the Giant King to Loki. 'Well, I can tell you now, it stretched a long, long, way away – right here in fact, all the way to the sea! I was trying to make you drink up the very sea itself, Thor! Not even the thirstiest of the giants could ever manage that! But I must say, you had a very good try.'

Thor's face was flushing like an ominous sunrise. His voice came out very low: 'And the cat?'

'Ah, that cat,' said the Giant King. 'You must realise by now, Thor, that in my realm nothing is quite what it seems to be. It's not a cat at all, that one – it's a snake. *The* snake, in fact – Jormungand, the one that circles and guards the whole of Middle Earth.'

This elegant bronze brooch is designed around a snake-like animal. Its intricate, coiled design is typical of Viking Age art.

The 'World Snake', Jormungand, was an important character in Norse mythology. It was said that he lay coiled right round Middle Earth, biting his own tail. Sometimes he writhed about and made violent storms in the ocean which surrounded the edge of Middle Earth.

'But that's total madness!' protested Thor. 'If I'd succeeded in lifting up the World Snake, I'd have destroyed everything!'

'That's very true,' said King Utgard-Loki. 'I must admit, I got quite concerned when you managed to get one of its paws right off the ground. No doubt you caused a nasty earthquake somewhere, by doing that. And now, no doubt, you are wondering who that old woman was that you wrestled at the end.'

Thor waited.

Thor, Loki and the children rowed to the land of the Giants and home again in a little wooden boat.

The Vikings were brilliant at building boats and ships which could sail long distances across rough seas. The boats caught the wind in their square sails, or were rowed by teams of oarsmen. They were beautifully shaped with long, curving lines and sweeping prows, often elaborately carved.

Small rowing boats were used for fishing and for shorter journeys along rivers, across lakes and around the coast. These boats are from Norway and were buried with a dead Viking ruler.

'She is not a giant,' said the King, 'and she is certainly not a god. I will give you a clue. She is the strongest creature in the whole world. No-one can overcome her. Every man and every woman is afraid of her coming, for once she arrives, no-one can drive her away, not until they are dead.'

He turned to Thialfi and Roskva. 'Well, are you any good at riddles? Can you guess her name?'

They shuddered at his description, but shook their heads.

'She is Old Age,' the Giant King said softly. 'Young as you are now, one day even you two will meet her. Then you will remember with sadness, how even mighty Thor could not destroy her.'

For a long moment, there was a seething silence. In the sky, dark storm clouds were gathering. Thor drew power from them. He took a firm grip on his hammer and swung it back, ready to strike a blow against the trickster Giant King.
But as the hammer sliced through the air, they were all suddenly blinded by a dazzling flash of light.

'Oh!' cried Roskva, 'he's gone! The Giant King – he's vanished!'

They all gazed around them. It was quite true.

Loki said in a weary voice, 'Come on Thor, let's admit it, the giants have made fools of the gods this time. I'm ready to go home.'

And he led the way down to the beach, and the boat that would take them safely back to Middle Earth.

Don't Play

Dangerous Games

A man once met a giant walking across his farm-land, and they got talking. After chatting about this and that for a while, the conversation turned to gambling games.

'When it comes to playing tables, there's no-one in all of Middle Earth who can beat me!' the farmer boasted.

'Is that so?' replied the giant. 'Well, in Jotunheim (where I come from), most of my friends would say that I was the champion. It sounds to me that you and I would be pretty well matched, my little friend. I tell you what – why don't we sit down now and play a game together?'

Well, on the one hand, the farmer wasn't at all keen: he knew that giants could be dangerous. On the other hand, it was years since he'd lost a game, and he was pretty sure he could always come out on top, no matter how skilled his opponent.

So, 'All right,' he said.

The giant waited while the farmer set up a gaming table in the yard. Then they both sat down.

'What prize shall we have for the winner?' the farmer wondered.

'No prize,' said the giant straight away. 'Instead, let's have a penalty for the loser: whoever loses the game must also lose his life!'

The farmer couldn't help thinking that these were rather drastic stakes, and he began to realise that the giant's friendliness was no more than a sham.

He stole a glance at the giant, who was chuckling to himself in a very sinister way. He looked much too big and fierce to argue with. So the farmer sighed and shook hands with him, and they began to play.

With Giants!

This is the type of game that the giant forced the farmer to gamble over. The square board is made of wood. Like many everyday Viking objects, it is decorated with elaborately carved patterns.

The board is marked out in seven rows of seven holes each, and would have had a set of bone or wooden pegs to fit into them. It may have been used to play a game similar to the modern 'Fox and Geese'.

The Norse Sagas called such games 'playing tables'. We know that they were very popular, since similar sets have been found buried in many Viking graves. Some contained different coloured glass playing pieces, some had both plain pieces and larger 'kings', and some included dice.

The game went on for a long time. They were both very clever players. But after a few hours, it came to an end – and the loser was the giant.

According to their agreement, the giant was now supposed to let the farmer cut his head off, or kill him in some other way. But it turned out that he was a coward.

'Don't kill me, please don't kill me yet!' begged the giant, holding up his enormous hands to protect himself. 'Whoah, just a minute. Spare my life, little fellow, and in return I'll give you a wonderful prize.'

'Oh yes?' said the farmer, fingering his sword. He could tell that the giant was as nervous as he was, for he had broken out into a pungent sweat. 'It had better be a good one.'

'Oh, it will be,' the giant promised him. His eye fell on the farmer's hut: it was very small, and badly in need of repair. 'I'll tell you what: how would you like a fine new house, eh? One that's fully furnished, and all nicely equipped for a lord?'

'That would be great!' said the farmer, hardly able to believe his ears. 'But how long do I have to wait for it?'

'Oh, not long at all,' promised the giant. 'In fact, I'll rush straight off and see to it now. It'll be ready by tomorrow.'

The next day, the farmer and his family woke up, and found to their amazement that their miserable old hut had indeed been transformed into a magnificent hall. The benches were all covered with woven cushions and furs, the chests were full of silver, and the store rooms were overflowing with good food.

His wife was well pleased, and so were their children.

'Just the same,' said his wife, 'I have a feeling that this is too good to be true.'

Sure enough, a few days later, the giant came back.

'Pleased with your house, old friend?'

'We're all delighted,' said the farmer.

'Fancy another game, then?'

At once, the farmer was on his guard. 'Well ... I can't say that I really do ...'

'Oh come on,' the giant urged him, 'what are you afraid of? You know no-one ever beats you! Just stop arguing and get the gaming table out again. This time we'll let the winner choose his prize without any messing about.'

When the farmer's family opened the storage chests inside their new hall, they were excited to find them brimming with treasure like this silver brooch. Norse people valued silver very highly. During the Viking Age, precious objects were often stolen in raids on towns, villages and monasteries all around the coasts of Europe.

Since the giant would not take 'no' for an answer, they sat down and played again. But this time, the luck turned – and the giant was the winner.

The farmer said gloomily, 'I suppose you'll claim a prize I can't afford, and I'll have to sell this lovely house to pay for it.'

'No, no, don't worry, you can keep the house – keep it for always,' said the giant. 'I've thought of a prize much more to my taste. I want you to give me your son to be my servant.'

'My son?' cried the farmer, jumping up in a terrible fright. 'My only boy? I can't give him to you.'

'Of course you can,' grinned the giant. 'Didn't I give you something really wonderful when you won? Well I'm the winner this time around, and fair's fair. I want your boy for my prize. We agreed before we started to play that the winner could choose: you can't back out of it now.'

'But,' said the farmer, thinking desperately, 'but ... but ... He's not here at the moment. He's out. Visiting.'

'Never mind,' said the giant, 'I'll come back for him tomorrow. Early tomorrow morning. Make sure you've got him ready for me.' Suddenly he pulled his enormous sword out of its sheath, and pointed it threateningly at the farmer's stomach. 'If I don't get what I'm entitled to, I might have to kill you instead!'

Viking times could be violent and dangerous, so it was common for a man to keep his sword with him. He carried it in a scabbard slung from a strap across his body, or hung from a belt around his waist.

Swordsmiths made swords by a complicated process of twisting and hammering bars of iron together in the hot forge. As a result, the finished blade was covered in beautiful, swirling patterns. It had a hard edge, and was so strong it would spring back into shape if bent. The hilt (handle) was made of wood, horn or bone, covered with soft sheepskin, cloth or leather to make it comfortable to grip.

Good swords were very valuable. Some were given special names such as 'Fierce' or 'Leg-Biter' and were passed down from father to son.

Odin's Trick

The farmer watched the giant walk away, clomping heavily over the hills. Then he fell onto his knees and began to cry and moan. He didn't know what to do. This son of his was only a young boy, and the farmer loved him dearly.

At last he went home and confessed everything to his wife. First she gave him a good telling off for gambling; then she had a good cry as well. But she pulled herself together and said,

'We're wasting time. If we're going to outwit this giant and save our poor boy, we might have to resort to magic. Only the gods can help us with that. Go out, you foolish man, and say a prayer to Odin. He's in charge of all the world's wisdom and magic, isn't he? If anyone can help us, it'll be him.'

So the farmer went off and prayed for many hours to Odin, the god who sees everything and can work the impossible. He prayed until night came. Then he went in, kissed his family goodnight, bolted his door and went to bed.

A wind blew up. When the darkness was thickest and the wind was wildest, someone came knocking.

This wooden carving from Norway shows a man with one eye. It is the god Odin, who gave away his other eye in exchange for a drink from the Fountain of Wisdom.

Odin, the 'All-Father' of the gods, was rather mysterious and frightening. He controlled poetry, wisdom, writing in runes and all spiritual matters, including death. He knew every secret in the world, and could prophesy the future. He could take the shape of any animal or bird, or disguise himself as a simple traveller. Everyone feared his powers – particularly in battle, when he often made the enemy blind, or paralysed with fear.

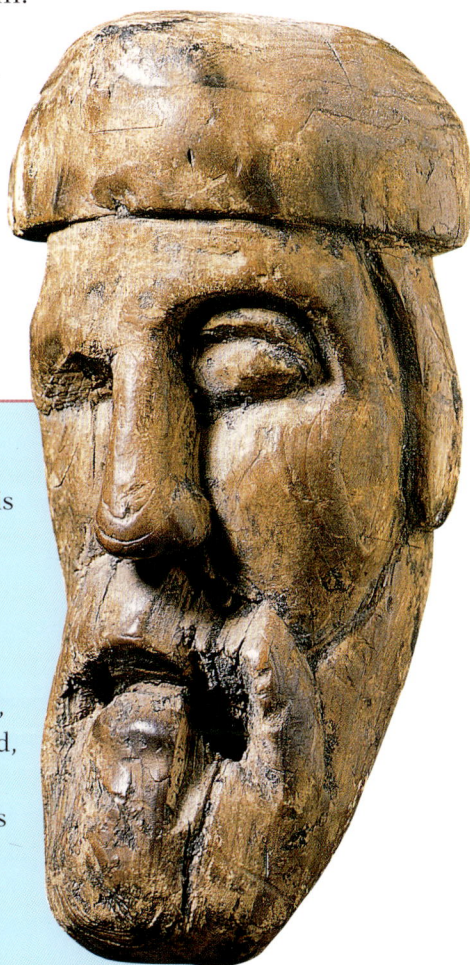

The farmer jumped up, quaking. 'Who's there?!' He was afraid that the giant had decided not to wait for morning.

A deep voice called back on the wind's breath, 'It is I! You called me and I have come. Open the door!'

The farmer opened it. There on the step stood a stranger. His cloak and his wide-brimmed hat were the dim blue colour of darkness. Mysteries wafted across his shadowed, one-eyed face. Two ravens sat on his shoulders, a wolf crouched at his feet, and behind him a sleek horse with eight legs stood tossing its mane.

The farmer whispered, 'My lord? ... Odin?'

'Give me your son,' said Odin. 'I have come to save him.'

The farmer carried the sleeping boy from his bed, and put him into the god's outstretched arms.

'Before morning,' said Odin, 'a whole field of barley will grow behind your house. I shall turn your son into a barley-grain and hide him in it. The giant will never find him there!'

The farmer opened his startled mouth to thank him; but the windy night had already swallowed Odin and his child.

Morning came. The farmer went out and saw that, just as Odin had promised, a big field of ripe barley had sprung up from nothing. While he was staring at it, he heard *clomp, clomp, clomp* – and there was the giant!

'That boy,' he said, leering. 'I've come to get him. Where is he?'

'I ... I don't know,' said the farmer truthfully. 'He's lost.'

The giant looked at the farmer. Then he looked very carefully at the barley field.

'You cheat!' he roared. 'This is magic! You've had the gods

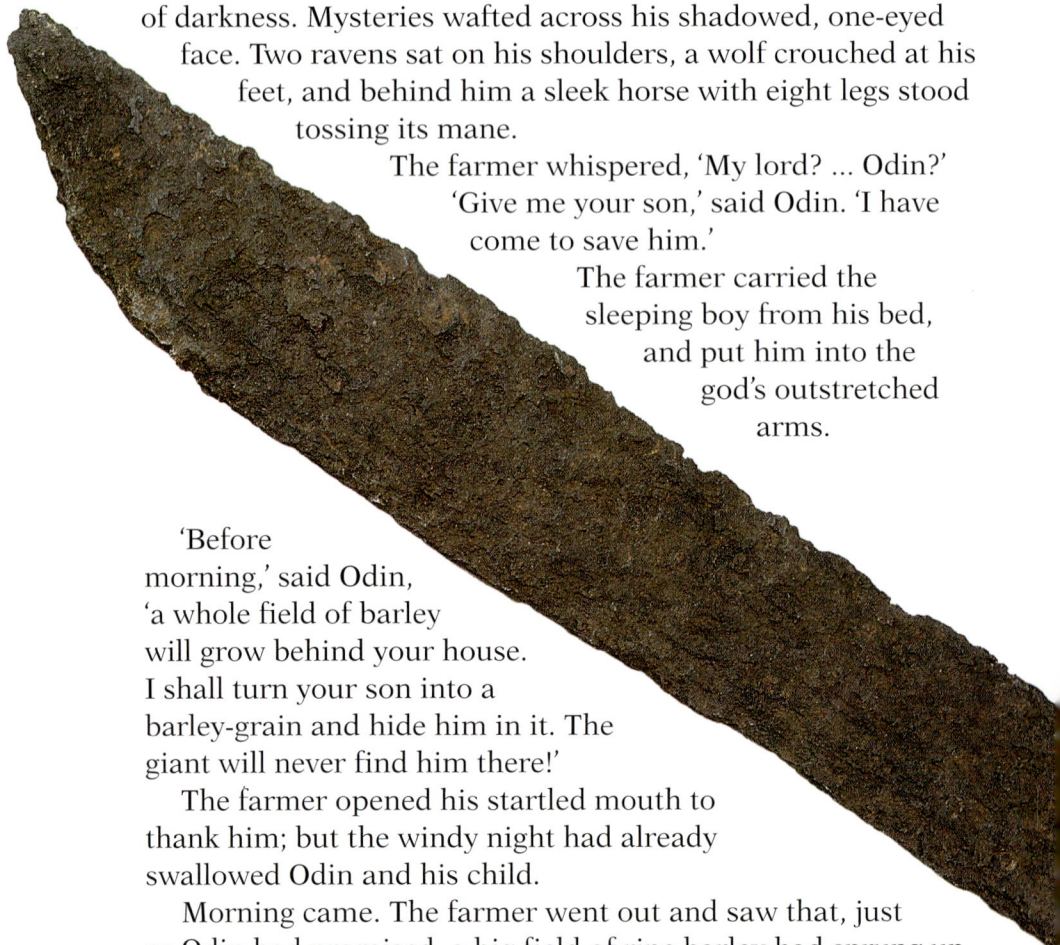

helping you, haven't you? Ahah, ohoh, don't think you can get away with this, you little maggot!'

He whirled round and, stooping low to get through the door, he blundered into the farmer's tool shed, thrashing around inside it until he came out waving a scythe.

'I'm going to use it to cut that field of barley right down – all of it – until I get my hands on the boy!'

There was nothing the farmer could do, except watch the giant helplessly. *Slash, slash, slash* – in no time at all, the whole field was scythed right down.

The giant stood in the middle of it, kicking the broken stalks. 'I know the kind of tricks those gods play,' he rasped. He threw down the scythe and pulled out his sword. 'I bet my lovely boy-prize is hidden in one of those ears of barley. Well, I'm going to slice them all in half until I find him!'

The day went on. The giant worked hard with his sword, slicing up the ears of barley, one by one. But the grains were very small: most of them slipped untouched to the ground. By nightfall the giant still had not found the boy, and he had to go home to sleep in Jotunheim without his prize.

The giant cut down the field of barley using a scythe like this, with a sharp iron blade. It would have had a long, upright wooden handle (unfortunately this one has rotted away over time). Scythes were important farm tools, used for cutting cereal crops or long grass to make hay. July-August was known as 'Haymaking Month' and August-September as 'Corn-Cutting Month'.

Most Viking Age people worked on the land. Some had their own farms, while poorer women and men worked as servants or slaves for the other farmers.

Under the cover of darkness, shrouded by the gale's din, Odin turned the boy back into his own shape and sent him safely home. The farmer found him on the doorstep, sitting on a stone; and on the stone were carved some runes, which said:

SEEK THE HELP OF OTHERS

'He's got no more time for us, I suppose,' said the farmer's wife, hugging her son tightly. 'He'll be too busy thinking about all that magic and wisdom of his. We'd better try one of the other gods. How about that Honir? I've always liked the sound of him. They say he's very strong and brave, and he's got a soft spot for ordinary people like us, since he had a hand in our creation.'

The farmer hesitated, in a terrible fluster.

'Go on!' urged his wife. 'We've got to do *something*, haven't we? Go out and try.'

Norse people wrote in 'runes'. The earliest runes appear in the second century AD, about 1,800 years ago. The Norse alphabet is known as the 'Futhark', and there were several different versions. Each of the 16 letters was a pattern of straight lines, designed to be cut with a knife into wood, metal or stone, for the Norse people did not use paper. The myths say that Odin discovered runes.

Viking Age rune stones have been found all over Scandinavia. A few survive in Britain and Ireland. Many were memorials to the dead. This one was made by a woman called Sigrid in memory of her husband Holmger. It is about 900 years old and comes from Ramsund in Sweden. The runes are written on the body of a snake-like animal.

Honir's Trick

So the farmer went out into the night, and called loudly on Honir to come down the rainbow-bridge from Asgard to help them. All night long his prayers were answered by silence. But at dawn the farmer opened his door – and there stood the tall, handsome god!

'Trust me with your son,' said Honir.

The farmer brought him the boy. Honir took his hand and began to run with him, pulling him behind, running, running, almost flying, until they reached the sea.

There in the sea, they saw seven white swans. Honir called to them, 'Come ashore!'

One swan stepped out on to the sand. As it came towards them, they heard the giant's footsteps, clomping angrily towards them over the hill.

But before the giant could reach them, Honir touched the boy and whispered secret words. The boy shimmered – and then vanished! Honir had turned him into a soft white feather, and hidden him on the swan's head.

The giant reached the sea-shore and the wretched farmer came panting up behind.

'He's in there, isn't he?' roared the giant. 'I bet you've hidden him inside that swan. Well ... if I can't get him alive, I'll just have to take him dead instead!'

And without further ado, he seized the swan in his big, rough hands and twisted its neck until it died.

The giant gave a cruel laugh. A sad cloud of feathers came tumbling down around him. Seizing the dead swan, he pushed the feathers aside and strode away.

One by one, the feathers came to earth. When the last one landed, the boy stepped out. The farmer clutched him, hardly able to believe he was still safe.

'If you ask me,' said Honir, 'that villain will be back again quite soon.'

'What shall I do, oh dear, whatever shall I do?' begged the desperate farmer.

'You need to settle this business once and for all,' said Honir.

'But I'm not clever enough to do that. You need the help of someone ruthless, a real expert in the arts of trickery. You know who I mean: it's Loki.'

Loki's Trick

The farmer was afraid to call on Loki. He'd heard all the usual tales about him: he knew it was dangerous to trust him. But Honir had gone now, and on the shore, standing by the grey sea, holding his boy, he felt very alone. He knew the giant would be back, as soon as he realised the boy had got away.

A voice behind him said,

'You should have called me in the first place, farmer. No-one understands the giants better than I do. That one you gambled with is no more than an idiot. It'll be as easy as blowing kisses to get rid of him. Lend me the boy, and I'll show you.'

The farmer whirled round. He couldn't see anyone.

Loki's voice called, 'On the sea, farmer!'

He turned the other way – and saw Loki, dancing darkly on the shifting shapes of the waves. The god ran over the water towards the boy, touched him, winked at him; and the boy was gone.

The farmer's heart jumped. 'Where is he?' he whispered.

'Under the sea,' laughed Loki, 'inside a fish. I've changed him into a tiny egg – a fish-roe. Ahah, but here comes our old friend, the giant.'

Clomp, clomp, clomp.

'I know what's happening!' roared the giant, as he came back over the hill. 'I know where the boy is! Well, I've brought a spear with me, farmer, and I'm going to do some fishing!'

He waded out deep into the sea, until it reached his towering thighs. 'Little boy,' he shouted, 'Here I come. Swim under my spear so I can eat you!'

Meanwhile, back on the beach, Loki said to the farmer, 'Why are you trembling? Pull yourself together man, and help me to dig.'

The giant may have used a gruesome pronged spear like this when he fished for the boy. Fishermen also used nets and hand-lines to catch fish in the sea, lakes and rivers.

Fish was an important part of the Viking Age diet. Sometimes it was salted and dried so that it kept for a long time without going bad. Afterwards it was eaten raw, smeared with butter. Freshly-caught fish was often baked, wrapped in grass, on red-hot stones.

Together, they dug with their bare hands in the soft white sand. Soon they had made a deep hole. They laid driftwood and seaweed over it until it was completely hidden.

By the time they had finished, the giant was splashing out of the sea, holding his barbed spear up high. Hanging from the prongs was a big fish.

'That's the one,' whispered Loki, poised like a wildcat. 'Watch him.'

The giant sat down and pulled out his knife. He slit the fish open: inside it lay a slippery bundle of pink eggs. One by one, he began to pull the eggs apart and hold them to the light.

'There!' he roared, 'I have him!'

Loki sprang forward. He leaped onto the giant, he knocked the egg out of his clumsy fingers. The egg fell onto the sand ...

'Change again!' Loki shrieked at it ...

... and it changed back into the boy.

'Run!' shouted Loki.

The boy sprang up and ran down the beach. The giant blundered after him. They came to the sand hole, hidden under the branches and seaweed. The boy dodged round it. But the giant pounded right over it – the cover gave way – and he fell in.

'Aaagh...!!' His furious roar faded away to silence.

'The hole is bottomless,' said Loki. 'He'll fall down and down, past the World Tree's roots, until he reaches the Realm of the Dead.'

He put an arm round the boy and slapped the farmer on the back. 'He's finished now. You're safe! *I* did it, Loki the cunning one!' His voice sank very low. 'Don't bother to thank me. But remember this, farmer – no-one can trust me to help them more than once. Next time, you might not be so lucky. Don't go playing games with giants again.'

Further reading

For children

John D. Clare, *I was There: Vikings*, Bodley Head

Kevin Crossley-Holland, *Axe-Age, Wolf-Age*, Andre Deutsch

Kathleen N. Daly, *Norse Mythology A-Z*, Facts on File

Michael Harrison and Tudor Humphries, *The Doom of the Gods*, Oxford University Press

Rosalind Kerven, *Sorcery and Gold*, Cambridge University Press

Roger Lancelyn Green, *Myths of the Norsemen*, Puffin Classics

David M. Wilson, *The Vikings Activity Book*, British Museum Press

British Museum Cut-Out Model: Viking Ship, British Museum Press

For adults

John Chadwick, *Reading the Past: Runes*, British Museum Press

Kevin Crossley-Holland, *The Norse Myths*, Penguin

James Graham-Campbell, *The Viking World*, Frances Lincoln

Jacqueline Simpson, *The Viking World*, Batsford

R. I. Page, *Norse Myths*, British Museum Press

R. I. Page, *Chronicles of the Vikings*, British Museum Press

Magnus Magnusson, *Vikings!*, Bodley Head/BBC

Sources of the pictures

Front cover: Carved head made from antler, Statens Historiska Museum, Stockholm, Sweden, inv. 22044

p. 4   Mythological 'map' of the Norse world: drawn by Catherine Wood.

p. 8   Wagon from Oseberg, Norway: University Museum of National
          Antiquities Oslo, Norway/Eirik Irgens Johnsen

p. 10   Bronze figurine of Thor: National Museum of Iceland, Reykjavik,
          Iceland/Ivar Brynjolfsson

p. 12   Furnace stone with face of Loki: Forhistorisk Museum Moesgård,
          Denmark/Fotograf Dehlholm

p. 15   Silver mask: Riksantikvarieambetet Och Statens Historiska Museer,
          Stockholm, Sweden

p. 18   Thor's hammer: The National Museum, Copenhagen, Denmark.

p. 21   Reconstruction of hall at Fyrkat: The National Museum,
          Copenhagen, Denmark

p. 23   Wooden scoop from Hedeby: Archäologisches Landesmuseum der
          Christian-Albrechts-Universität, Schloss Gottorf, Germany

p. 25   Ox horn carved with runes: Archaeological Museum, Stavanger,
          Norway

p. 29   Bronze openwork brooch: By courtesy of the Trustees of the British
          Museum, MLA 1982.6-2.1

p. 30   Boats from Gokstad: University Museum of National Antiquities
          Oslo, Norway

p. 33   Viking gaming board: National Museum of Ireland, Dublin, Ireland

p. 35   Silver brooch: By courtesy of the Trustees of the British Museum,
          MLA 1901.7-18.1

p. 36   Sword: By courtesy of the Trustees of the British Museum, MLA
          87.2-9.1

p. 37   Wooden head of Odin: University Museum of National Antiquities
          Oslo, Norway/Ove Holst

p. 38-9   Scythe: By courtesy of the Trustees of the British Museum, MLA
          1912.7-23.3

p. 40-1   Runestone: Antikvarist-Topografiska Arkivet (ATA), Stockholm,
          Sweden/Bernt. A. Lundberg

p. 44   Iron leister (fish-spear): Museum of Natural History and
          Archaeology, Norwegian University of Science and Technology,
          Trondheim, Norway